Copyright © 2014 B.B. Steele
All rights reserved.

ISBN: 0615860362
ISBN 13: 9780615860367

Library of Congress Control Number: 2013920185

"If you can dream it, you can do it"

-Walt Disney

This book is dedicated to Aaron, Morgan, Nathaniel, Jake, Tylor, Zachary, Jessica, Anna, Ruthie, Sara, Isaiah, Eli, Jenessa, Aubrey, Addison, Emerson, Cyrus.

I would like to thank the people who helped with this book. Robin Whaley, Cathy and Steven Dronen, Julie Bono, Mary Snyder. I love you all.

If I could I would get in my big red balloon and go back in time. I would explore all the wonders that float around in my mind.

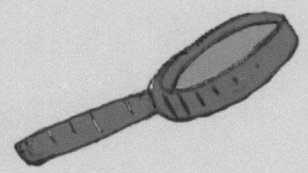

I would start with the dinosaurs and explore how they came to be. How long were they here and why did they have to leave.

I would climb the tallest mountain to see what was on top. I would throw hellos down its rocky slopes and wonder just how far they dropped.

I would build myself a boat and off I would be, exploring and sailing the deep blue seas.

I would find a camel tall and lean with extra big humps so I could sit atop and sing. I would travel the desert day and night and stop by the pyramids to be polite.

I would find a rocket ship fast and swift that would take me to the moon and back lickety-split.

If I could I would do all the things I dream of everyday, but they will have to wait. Meeting dinosaurs, climbing mountains, exploring pyramids and sailing the deep blue seas makes the moon rock me fast asleep.

B.B. Steele lives and grew up in The Great Smoky Mountains of East Tennessee. With the beauty of the mountains around her, inspiration for her writing is not hard to find. This is B.B Steele's first children's book and proof that with faith in God, hard work, and believing in yourself dreams can come true.

B.B. Steele, Sevierville, Tennessee USA

auntbbsteele@gmail.com

www.ingramcontent.com/pod-product-compliance
Lightning Source LLC
Chambersburg PA
CBHW042120040426
42449CB00002B/123